Memoirs
Selected Poems

Memoirs
Selected Poems

Rebekah Kenton

KS Books Ltd, London

www.ksbooksltd.com
E-mail: info@ksbooksltd.com

First published in 2025 by KS Books Ltd
Copyright © Rebekah Kenton 2025

The moral right of the author has been asserted.
All rights reserved.

No part of this publication may be reproduced, stored in a retrieval system or transmitted, in any form or by any means, without the prior permission in writing of the publisher, nor be circulated in any form of binding or cover other than that in which it is published and without a similar condition including this condition being imposed on the subsequent purchaser.

A CIP catalogue record for this book is available from the British Library.

ISBN 978-1-917606-33-2

Book design by Chris Demers
Front cover image by Rebekah Kenton

For Ritva

Contents

ACKNOWLEDGEMENTS ... 10

AWAKENING

THE OUTER COURT ... 12

RAINBOW ... 13

A CONCERT ... 14

ANOTHER CUP ... 15

LETTER-BOMB ... 16

SPANISH COFFEE ... 17

PROFIT ... 18

A STORM ... 19

HEALING ... 20

NO SUGAR ... 21

MY TEACHER ... 22

RETREAT

PURIFICATION OF EARTH ... 24

PURIFICATION OF WATER ... 25

PURIFICATION OF AIR ... 26

PURIFICATION OF FIRE ... 27

SLEEPLESS NIGHTS ... 28

THE WALL ... 29

SILENT ILLUMINATION ... 30

BEYOND CLOCKS	31
LANDSCAPE GAZING	32
SOUVENIR	33
TEA PARTY	34

THE GARDENS OF LONDON

THE CHAMBER OF NATURE	36
WATERLOW PARK	37
HYDE PARK	38
WOODCHURCH ROAD	39
MARESFIELD GARDENS	40
THE ROSE GARDEN	41
RUSSELL SQUARE	42
HAMPSTEAD HEATH	43
BATTERSEA PARK	44
LANSDOWNE ROAD	45
PAULTON'S SQUARE	46
HIGHGATE CEMETERY	47
RIVER THAMES	48

THE DARK NIGHT

THE SUN	50
THE FULL MOON	51
MERCURY RETROGRADE	52

VENUS	53
MARS	54
JUPITER	55
SATURN	56
CHIRON RETURN	57
URANUS	58
NEPTUNE	59
PLUTO	60
IF YOU PRAY	61
THE INNER TREE	62
THE GATE	63

ODD THOUGHTS

THE SKY AT NIGHT	66
HISSTORY	67
THE PYRAMID	68
A CONFERENCE	69
REGENT'S COLLEGE	70
GREAT ESCAPE	71
FAMILY TREE	72
WHAT THEN	73
LANDSCAPES OF THE SOUL	74

ODD THOUGHTS	75

OLD AGE

THE HARVEST MOON	78
DANGEROUSLY OLD	79
DREAM	80
THE WARDROBE	81
THE PHOTO ALBUM	82
MY MOTHER	83
LIFETIME	84
GOOD LUCK	85
LOST FUTURE	86
LESSON	87
HOUSE OF BOOKS	88
THE GAME	89
THE JOURNEY	90

ACKNOWLEDGEMENTS

I would like to thank my Finnish poetry teachers Matti Paavilainen, Risto Ahti and Väinö Kirstinä for their encouragement and advice. I am grateful to the librarians Eeva Puro and Ritva Piispanen for arranging literary events and meetings.

I am greatly indebted to my husband Warren Kenton (Z'ev ben Shimon Halevi) and my Buddhist teacher John Crook (Chuan-deng Jingdi) for their spiritual knowledge, wisdom and understanding.

Many thanks to my friends Lesley Beck, David Coussell and Alison Roberts for their support and help with editing and Chris Demers for the book design.

AWAKENING

THE OUTER COURT

The lecture took place in a room
just above the street level.

No coffee was served.
There were only books for sale.
I was so thirsty.
Although the old man read his lecture
from a paper,
I heard it as if it was
the oral tradition.

His words did not comfort my thirst.
They burnt like hot spices.
He spoke about the gravity
of my situation,
telling me that I was lost in a wilderness
without a map or a guide.

RAINBOW

When the heart wakes up, the formal exercise is over
and it is time to practise with live ammunition.
An open heart is an easy target.
It is constantly being hit and moved by sharp images.
The street is not what it used to be.
No defences
work against this onslaught of impressions.
Heaven looks at me with blue eyes
and there is nothing personal about it.

Simultaneous sunshine and showers
produced a rainbow.
Take note, and let your laughter and tears
flow freely!
Who knows what kind of arrow is
being shot with that bow?

If you are the target,
there is no escape, no safe distance.
Forget the exercise!

A CONCERT

The music starts green,
but soon it sounds like
the entire rainbow.

It does not matter how many nadis
there are in your subtle body.
The Maestro plays all of them
as you are nothing but an echo
of his instrument,
a resonating radiance.

But the Gardener
makes a simple statement.
He says it all
in just the top and base notes;
white and red
carnations.

ANOTHER CUP

At the lower levels of the universe
the cup is definitely half empty.
Only a fool would insist that it is half full.
Is optimism permissible at all in a suffering world?
Young wine did not have much character,
but my mature years are more interesting.

Not so with coffee.
You have to drink it fresh and quickly.
Any leftovers taste bitter
like a missed opportunity.
Wake up before bitterness gets hold of you!
There is an awful lot of it about.

Transformation is only one step away,
upwards, not sideways.
Sideways is more of the same
and one gets lost easily.
One can look the other way, fall asleep
and lose the rest of the day.
It will not come back.
You must start again
with a fresh cup of coffee.

LETTER-BOMB

The letter-bomb exploded in my heart.
Don't come, he wrote, circumstances have changed
and you are no longer welcome.

Never has coffee tasted so black, the lesson so bitter.
But I learnt quickly. Don't count on friends,
especially the dearest ones.
Nothing personal, circumstances have changed.

Time moves on relentlessly
like a river, years passing by.
When did I become middle-aged?
I did not notice the shift.
Maturity is not a revelation, it is a long process.
A single letter-bomb can shatter the foundation
and one has to start again. What for?

SPANISH COFFEE

How can I ever take coffee literally
after it opened my eyes to see
the inside of the cup.

What role does the plate have
in this coffee ceremony?
Forget duality for a while!
Appearances are deceptive
when different pieces come together.

The Spanish coffee was double strong.
Maybe because I was only a traveller there
my mind was elevated.
The Pyrenees still hold traces of ancient mule tracks,
where merchants crossed the mountains
laden with books, some of them not yet written.

I have not yet written out the Spain
that nearly took my life
and then gave it back, in a different form.
I have not been the same since.

PROFIT

Coffee is an excellent washing liquid
for grey feelings, a tired mind.
It restores colours to their original meaning
as if the eyes had been cleansed from the inside.

There are purists who warn about damage to the nerves.
What then is ideal health? My soul would not survive
the dullness of a single decaffeinated day.
For the price of a cup of coffee
the profit is enormous.
I pay willingly and become rich,
this is how I run my business.

I have to account for every day.
Daydreams make a loss,
but the moments spent awake
add up to a fortune.

A STORM

What started this storm in my coffee cup?
It was there at breakfast,
after a dream which I can't quite remember.
Maybe I was told something
that I did not want to hear.

By mid morning I was being tossed around
by invisible forces
like a piece of paper in a tempest,
my mind full of thunder and lightning.

What are my concealed passions
compared with the silent screams
of the flowers?
What are my private tears
compared with the public downpour
of the heavens?
As inside, so outside.

HEALING

The daydream was so good
that it was worth seeing it over and over again.
It was in fact a nightmare hard to escape from.
For such an affliction there is only one remedy,
a cup of coffee in a café.
This medicine never fails.

A lot of healing is taking place.
At last there is enough silence
for the truth to be heard.
I am peeling off dreams that are no longer needed
like bandages from a wound
that needs no more protection.

NO SUGAR

No sugar, please. And no cake either.
I want my coffee pure and strong.
That is good for the heart.

A breakthrough. There is light.
My face feels almost invisible
and my smile so deep that
it does not show on the surface.

The conclusion from my studies is
that conscious love
does not need added sugar.

MY TEACHER

Your pen is a flute.
It makes silent paper sing.
The echo of your voice
still travels through my heart
and blows away my lament.
Your flute blows away my lament.

Your pen is a candle.
It is burning away
the darkness of my thoughts.
Now your words are aflame
in my mind.
Your words are still burning in my mind.

Your pen is a stick
that breaks my illusions.
Ouch, how it hurts!
Now I do understand
what you said.
The meaning of what you said.

Your pen is a magic wand.
The power of your words
is changing my world.
Your pen is rewriting my life.
Rewriting the story of my life.

RETREAT

PURIFICATION OF EARTH

The walls I built around myself
became a prison.
I had to dismantle my fortress
brick by brick
until all was ground to dust and
I was free to go.

What I gave up
was not even mine.
Now my way is a path
in Your Garden
where every tree is sacred
and every grain of sand
is a precious stone.

PURIFICATION OF WATER

Sometimes water needs to be purified
by using poisonous substances. It hurts.
I do repent.
Whatever pain I caused
has now been given back to me,
generously.

How I managed to extract
this clean drop of water
from the murky pool of my feelings
I do not know,
but take it as an offering.
My tears are no longer salty
but sweet.

PURIFICATION OF AIR

My thoughts were like a flock of parrots,
clever and noisy, tearing things apart
but only building their own nests.

From a height where no bird can fly
came Your Wind
and blew away my thoughts.
Into this vacant space fell silence
softly, like snow,
each snow-flake radiant like an angel.

PURIFICATION OF FIRE

All prayer flags and prayer books
are eternally consumed in Your eyes
as You read our secrets.

Who am I to argue?
I surrender.
You have taken away everything else,
so please now also take this flame
that is no longer me
from the seat of its solitary meditation.

SLEEPLESS NIGHTS

Ah, sleepless nights
inside an old farmhouse
somewhere in a Welsh landscape.
The air is dense with ghosts,
the dark side of thoughts and feelings
barely moving at all.

The ancient pillow
filled with headaches and tears
is of no comfort.

Ah, sleepless nights
cocooned in a sleeping bag.
Waiting for transformation,
that moment of emptiness
before wings start to grow.

THE WALL

It is my task to extract clarity
from this blank wall.

My shadow gets in the way.
Zazen on a tightrope.
It is easy to fall off the cushion
into the abyss of the mind.
Another day of torment.

But I persevere
until the wall is alive
like the polished surface
of a sacred ornament.

SILENT ILLUMINATION

I lost words to describe it.
I lost hope for miracles.
I lost fear of failure.
I lost ambition for
enlightenment.

Now that rubbish is burning slowly
in an interior bonfire.
I am being cooked.
What into what?
I don't know
yet.

BEYOND CLOCKS

I was there. It came to me.
That sunset appeared from nowhere.
Earthly gold and purple
are but a cheap imitation
of that splendour.

I was in a time beyond clocks.
All time is there
all the time.

LANDSCAPE GAZING

*"Don't flow into the landscape.
Let the landscape come to you."*
The Wise One has spoken.

Suddenly I discover my eyes,
a new toy for a great experiment.
The view fades in and out of focus,
the hillside still and moving.
Heaven no longer out of reach.
The clouds are interesting
but give no answer.

What will happen here
after I have gone home?
Maybe a sheep, maybe a bird
will stop and look.

SOUVENIR

The guardian spirit of the stream
did not allow me
to take pebbles as souvenirs.
The stream did not want to lose
its precious stones.

The spirit said nothing
about the grass on the bank.
Now the dried stalks
decorate my altar
amongst other treasures.
The essence of those memories
quietly present,
invisible incense.

TEA PARTY

The water was once an early morning mist
and it is still magic.
Mixed with tea, served with cakes
in the garden,
it becomes miraculous.

The same miracle
in twenty different cups.

Some mysterious ingredient
makes love arise from my heart
like an early morning mist
and descend
on these trees, nettles, stones,
people.

THE GARDENS OF LONDON

THE CHAMBER OF NATURE

Nature's door is always open,
open for you and me to enter.
Enter into a magic landscape,
the land of fairies, elves and undines.
Let us go and find their castle,
castle hidden and protected.

Look behind those willow curtains.
Curtains and carpets all green-woven.
Woven into lace is the moss on the table,
table of the trolls both small and grown-ups.
Blue is the ceiling of that sacred chamber,
chamber of secret whispers and laughter.

Trees are standing tall and quiet.
Quiet are the watchers on the border.
Border into another kingdom,
kingdom of inner riches and beauties.
Paradise is always open,
open for you and me to enter.

WATERLOW PARK

Sometimes the sky looks
like watercolour paper
primed with a dirty brush,
when my grey mood
cuts off the sunshine.

How am I to make
this day memorable?
I don't want to waste it
as a blank page in my diary.

I once drowned in watercolour
but this time green, green,
mixed with yellow and blue.
How peacefully I sank
into the sea of Nature.

HYDE PARK

The scene of fatal meetings.
In the privacy of an open space
marriages are agreed
or separations declared,
Heaven being the only witness.

We all walk here in the company
of the Lords of Karma,
the gardeners of the soul.
Not a word is missed.
They listen and record our conversations
into the Book of Life and Death
as they make plans for the next season.

Some would regard the yarrow as a weed.
For those who know
it is a herb of medicine.

WOODCHURCH ROAD

The screams of the foxes
in the dark
are but a faint echo of
the sounds of an African night.

In Africa things grow differently.
You inherited the green fingers
of a jungle.
It is evident in this magic garden.
First nothing grew here,
but then they started to come
of their own accord.
Elder trees and lilacs
chose their places and stayed.

While it is true that for twenty years
you processed the soil,
externally and internally,
with skilful composting and trusting,
it still does not explain
why the air is so tangible
with growth and wellbeing,
as if all the devas of the neighbourhood
were trying to move in.

A ritual under a maple tree:
a bonfire
is but a pale imitation
of the fire of an African night.

MARESFIELD GARDENS

Sigmund Freud used to walk his dog
under these trees.

What a pity we never met.
I would have loved to
lie on your couch.
Anybody can solve my problems,
but who else would listen to
my dreams?

As an archaeologist
you dug deeper than
the antique shops of Vienna.
You went down to the burial sites
of the underworld.

Yet sublimation remains a mystery.
If I had been invited
as a guest to your house,
we would have sat in the library
and found the right book,
but maybe not
the answer.

THE ROSE GARDEN

Not just Truth, Goodness and Beauty.
The roses can express many things.
Congratulations!
Deepest condolences!
Thank you!
Sorry!
Get better!

A childhood friend wrote
in my ruled notebook:
"Beware, young lady, when you pick
the roses of life.
Even the most beautiful one
hides a stinging thorn."

How appropriate is
the statue of an archer here.
Hit and wounded by arrows,
divine or otherwise,
one is constantly seeking
healing.

RUSSELL SQUARE

Under mature trees
it is good to recover from
the history lesson of the British Museum.

Someone like myself
would have used those sewing needles
in ancient Egypt
or polished that bronze mirror.

I am contemplating my personal history,
burnt letters and diaries,
irretrievable memories.
Even the monuments of my youth
the cinema, the café and the dance hall
were all burnt down
and the school was demolished.

When I moved I sold my bed.
Whoever sleeps in it now
may have strange dreams,
but there is no record of
my thoughts or feelings
or who else was present.

The Book of Changes knows:
"A wanderer is one who seeks.
Strange lands and separation
are the wanderer's lot."

HAMPSTEAD HEATH

With zoom binoculars
I can see near and far.
On this hill
the glacier came to a halt.

I look back
to my early years in Finland
from where the Ice Age
never quite disappeared.
It was as if our bones
were sculpted from ice
and we were frozen in time
in some prehistoric permafrost
preserved by our Mothers,
the Snow Queens.

BATTERSEA PARK

The division between East and West
becomes irrelevant
at the meeting place
of the Peace Pagoda.

I must take a deep breath
when the Buddha's golden smile
transcends my understanding.
When does enlightenment begin
and where does it end?

Once a thunderbolt
illuminated a lotus
emerging from the marshland.

While I am waiting for
its petals to unfold,
I repeat my mantra
until it flows incessantly
like the River Thames
towards the Sea.

LANSDOWNE ROAD

The cat owns the garden and
two flats in the house,
her first and second homes.
She has her own entrance
and she comes and goes as she pleases.

Often you can see her furry face
at the window,
watching.
A brindled cat,
maybe not pretty but
she makes the most of her looks.

She is utterly spoilt
and her table manners are unspeakable.
She will drink your tea
when you look the other way.

Yet she is a very important cat,
the companion of a writer.
On a metaphysical manuscript
you may just see
her proud paw mark.

PAULTON'S SQUARE

People of destiny may pass away
but their gardens remain.
Their books, the orchards of imagination,
feed many generations,
and new layers grow
organically
as the myth changes form.

HIGHGATE CEMETERY

Whoever planted the cedar of Lebanon
would not recognise it
now, three hundred years later.
The park has gone
and the cedar overlooks
the Avenue of the Dead.

The landscape is ever changing.
Those buried here
knew a different London.
Time has lost its spell,
but the symbols of death on family vaults
are immortal.

Even familiar plants
look otherworldly here
as if they had seen too many ghosts
picking flowers with their misty fingers.

The final burial ceremony was
not the one conducted by a priest
but Mother Nature covering the tombs
with a green shroud.

RIVER THAMES

Occasionally you can just hear
a hidden tributary
under a street
or gaze into a calm canal.
All this water is slowly
flowing towards the River.

Like a serpent uncoiled
the River surges through
the body of London.
The currents and undercurrents
of its waters
generate a power
that is unstoppable,
awesome.

One cannot control
the river of life.
It carries your boat,
but how you navigate
is up to you.

THE DARK NIGHT

THE SUN

Active sun, far too active.
When you discharge your rage,
the weight of a thousand thunderstorms
descends upon my soul at once
but no relief.

My self is not spotless either,
but flares up, burns up,
layer after layer,
until the real fuel is exposed.
Is this the truth about myself?

My celestial time-keeper!
When you have counted my days to the end,
will there be a radiant supernova,
a moment of enlightenment,
before I disappear
from the wheel of my horoscope?

THE FULL MOON

I can't sleep. The night is not safe.
There is too much light on the wrong side.
The dreaded north is revealed.
In the moving tides
the eternal ice of permafrost is rising,
the snowflakes of my ancestors now unburied.

The hidden face of my ego is always unripe
like the north side of an apple.
There is something false
about my tears reflecting this unreal light,
this indoor fountain
endlessly recycling the same waters.

Where shall I go
for advice?

MERCURY RETROGRADE

We are not thinking at the same frequency.
Our words do not reach very far
and they are only half understood.

The messenger is late.
The message is lost.
I will never know what was in that letter
if it was not sent,
especially if it was never written.

No news
was not good news after all.

VENUS

Your temptations are endless
like a forest, green upon green.
When I get lost, at least I know where I am.
But I was not supposed to be here!

Danger! My thirst is deeper
than your wine.

MARS

One step wrong and you struck me down.
Accident-prone, says the book.

My body curls up like an injured lizard
while the reptilian brain plans its survival strategy.
The journey from bed to kitchen
seems like ten miles.
How will I ever get there?

Past, present and future fears
will catch me in their net
if I don't dare to look.
The dark is invisible
and more frightening than red-hot flames.
Anger is hell. I have been there.
But the way of suffering is much longer,
much longer.

JUPITER

You open the soul to Love
but you never close the doors.
An open heart is an easy target
for despair.

You send Hope to stalk me
and it does not leave me alone.
It believes the impossible
and sees what is not.

Your good luck is a mirage.
Sunset clouds have golden edges
but the nightfall is inevitable.

All of us who ever loved you
are left with shining begging-bowls
full of empty promises.

SATURN

Slow down the music
and it becomes a lament.
Slow down the dance and it stops.
You are the end of earthly pleasures
and heavenly delights alike.

Your rings are shackles, not haloes.
You punish first.
Only later you let me understand
where I broke your law.
My crime? That my best
is not good enough.

CHIRON RETURN

Your wounded myth is
to be read with the inner eye.

On your return,
your message was a koan.
It took me three nights' sleep
to crack it.

What a fool I had been
to build all these sanctuaries for myself.
My intellectual and emotional structures
dissolved
when I saw the heavenly wheels turn
regardless of my belief systems.

There is no such thing as security,
said my teacher.

URANUS

Why do you create chaos out of order?
An earthquake is not the answer.
My life is in ruins once again
and there is your stamp
on every broken brick.

Of course you win the argument
with the high voltage
of your voice.

NEPTUNE

Here and there, now and then
are so closely connected
that there is no escape,
the burden of expanded consciousness.
You make me forget what I need to know
and remember what I don't want to know.

Ah, give me back my certainty
where numbers mean prices, not values.
When the inner becomes bigger than the outer,
containers get blurred and
the focus is lost.

Princes and Patriarchs bow
in front of the icon,
but the saint has moved on.
Miracles may still occur
there and here, then and now.

PLUTO

In your cauldron of transmutation
you extinguished my spiritual greed,
my desire to know the unknowable.
Now I can only whisper.
What lies beyond your veil is too vast
to be spoken aloud.

Thus you prepare me
for a solitude that is more lonely
than a zero.

IF YOU PRAY

If you pray for me, my friend,
ask for strength to endure
the dark heavens and hells.

Pray for some clarity, night-vision,
and a good harvest of wisdom and understanding.

If you pray for me, my friend,
do not say anything.
Just burn incense quietly,
scent and smoke interwoven
like my thoughts with yours
ascending.

THE INNER TREE

In the great stillness of hibernation
the bitter juices of the earth
are transformed into sweet sap.

When it is time to retire
into illness,
I drop all expressions from my face
like dead leaves
and go to that stillness
through my annular rings
into a centre point,
into a time when life was
as yet without form.

In this space I straighten my spine,
as a signpost
from earth to heaven.

THE GATE

That which is coming
is taking a long time to enter.
I need all my strength
to hold the gate open.

What is coming
is bigger than the wind
and more invisible.
It does not turn the leaves
of my tree.

It may already be in the house,
waiting for me
while I am still busy
at the gate.

My efforts are futile,
yet necessary.
Without an invitation
it would not come.

It has been here before
and may know me better
than I know myself.
More than anything in this world
I welcome the Presence.

ODD THOUGHTS

THE SKY AT NIGHT

The Earth may not count
even as a speck of pollen
within the cosmic flower
of the Milky Way.
Out there could be a whole garden
full of such flowers,
blooming and withering.

The choreography of Shiva's dance
is written somewhere.
I try to follow the footsteps
with binoculars,
but the stage is too large
for me to comprehend
from the box seat of our balcony.

I was told by a shooting star:
the real fulfilment
of your deepest wish
is to give it up.

HISSTORY

History is largely his story.

Hers is a story of
the hidden goddess.
Her victories are not recorded
in hisstory books.
Her naked power has been covered up
in mysteries.

Her jewellery is scattered around the world
in museums and private treasures.
Her dresses burst into flowers.
Her perfumes are made
in Paradise.

The goddess is learning
how to hiss.

THE PYRAMID

Who invented the pyramid and why?
Was it by trial and error,
or did somebody get the design
from the World of Ideas?
Was it a superhuman copy
of a mountain?
An attempt to reach
from earth to the heavens?

Even the "how" is not known.
Nor is "when".
The pyramid stands
like a monument to forgetfulness.

A CONFERENCE

Centuries of learning are summed up in two days. If you know, it is enough. If not, you go on digging into archives forgetting that history is not something else. It is ever moving on, filling up the time given to each of us.

Some make a contribution and others only take. I suppose they will pay later. The Great Work employs us all eventually and then there are no more holidays, only work and after-work. Why did these people come from all over the world? Knowledge can only be absorbed with love. Critics fall ill with indigestion and get nothing. Being a know-all is dangerous.

It takes courage to talk about God in a world where material thinking prevails. This conference is a moment to stop in front of a window and see how light comes in through the curtains. This knowledge bears the light in flaming letters. Much depends on how they are read and heard. Don't dismiss the words of wisdom. They could be the bridge to the landscape of the soul, where all this is known already. Don't let your personal view eclipse the overview.

In a curious way the soul depends on the ordinary mind.

REGENT'S COLLEGE

This is how I want
my picture taken:
on a misty October morning
against the vine-covered school building.

Old souls are always in training.
They give up
their weekend rest for study,
in order to be ready
for the Monday morning examination.

This is how I would like
my portrait painted:
as a still life in the class room
with my companions.

Walking around the inner courtyard
deepens my thoughts.
This is how I am sketching
my self-portrait:
my soul visible against the background
of the cloister.

GREAT ESCAPE

The escape route goes through the back streets. The flowers look natural. The way is otherwise grey, paved with mixed slates and cracks, there is a risk of falling over. A cat looks up surprised to see me at this time of the day.

My day is not my own. It belongs to real and imaginary duties. There is the work undone and eternal guilt. My interior space has been invaded. The office is overloaded. There is only one escape, out through the door.

A stolen moment, not borrowed. A table with just a cup on it but no papers. I must quickly refresh myself and drink the sunrays from the cup before they disappear. Life is asking me and I have to answer. The game is hide and seek. Who am I? I don't dare to think in case that inner child wakes up in tears. Will it ever grow up? Who would like to remember all those growing pains? I keep my tears private and don't shed them in public.

It is necessary to retrace my steps when privacy becomes unbearable and to go back to the safe routine of paperwork. Numbers are clean and free of feelings, a welcome break to escape from myself.

FAMILY TREE

Sometimes a family tree
drops its fruit
on the other side of the fence,
abroad.
It is easier to feel alien
in a foreign country
than at home.

In the winter many trees
look dead.
One has to trust
the process of growth.
Despair is a nursery
for new shoots.

However, there comes a time
to give up suffering.
It is not possible
to climb a Ladder
with crutches.

WHAT THEN

What then,
when you have gone so far
that you are only a name
and your name is only a word?
When all your colours have faded
and I no longer miss you,
what then is the purpose of life?

LANDSCAPES OF THE SOUL

Am Zuckerberg was my first address abroad,
in this life.
I walked downhill every morning
and up again in the evening, for months,
until I started dreaming in a foreign tongue.

Are these old picture books mine? Or someone else's?
All the same, all too familiar
are the images of many lives and cities,
as if they were the dark outlines
of my personal portraits.

The streets of Toledo were once red
like borders between countries on the map,
drawn with blood, the most expensive colour.
My soul's inheritance is this old Europe
spread out like a patched quilt
threadbare, torn, mended.

And yet, I had to escape
the forest of human relationships
into the desert, to remember myself.
In the light of a primordial sunrise
the horizon was unbroken
like a long uninterrupted thought.

ODD THOUGHTS

A thought after the afterthought.
*
My shadow in someone else's picture.
*
Your greatest weakness is your greatest strength.
*
A fate is an enquiry into what is possible and what is not.
*
It is said that God perceives His creation
through human consciousness.
Maybe He also enjoys the view
through a bird's eyes or a tree's senses.
*
Surely God must have created the scent first
before giving the plant a form and a name.
*
When the wind was shaking the Tree of Knowledge,
the words fell down as full sentences that made sense.
*
A round clockface shows the past, present and future
of the daily cycle.
A digital clock shows only the present number.
Which one is quality time?
*
Time itself is neutral.
It is we who make it sacred or secular.

*

The path of integrity is not a highway.
It is private for each person.
If the path is not used,
it overgrows very quickly.

*

Most important events happen in solitude.

*

Don't be fooled by slow motion.
Saturn does not wait.
Either you learn your lesson or you don't.

*

Icons and diagrams are views
into another garden where ideas are cultivated.

*

When the evening draws its black curtains
across the window
there is much to reflect.

*

Love is not measured.
It is given until your cup overflows,
or not given at all.

OLD AGE

THE HARVEST MOON

I was conceived under the Harvest Moon
in another place.
Now the same Moon rises
over the garden walls of London.
It is a heavy weight
that pulls up strange feelings
from a hidden well
in the depths of an Abyss.

Now I am the harvest.

DANGEROUSLY OLD

We are now dangerously old.
A generation of flower children
are withering.

The Christmas card address list
becomes shorter.
Birthdays are missing from the diary.
Friends have been deleted
from our lives.

What did Fate expect from us?

One by one we say
our last words. Final goodbyes.
After the last breath,
silence.

DREAM

The evening is resting
on my face.
Twilight settles in.
I am ready to fall asleep
into a dream
where my beloved is waiting.

Together we will explore
the paths of Paradise
and our dreams
will become visions.

THE WARDROBE

1950s. No dress shop in the village.
The lady measured me once a year
for a new outfit.
The rest was second-hand
from older children.
I was growing fast.

1960s. Still no shop in the village.
Fashions changed.
I had to make
my own miniskirts and flared trousers
with my own designs and patterns.

1970s. Times changed.
Got a job, moved to a city.
Had money but no time
to make clothes.
Plenty of shops to explore
for imported and exotic styles.

1980s etc. No comment. See photos.

By now I have undressed
those vanities. Almost.
What shall I wear
for my funeral?

THE PHOTO ALBUM

My long life recorded in pictures.
The child, the teenager, the adult.
Posing for portraits and group photos.
Jolly parties. Big smiles.
Snapshots of tourist attractions.
It looks like a good and happy life.
The camera does not lie.

But there are gaps.
No photos of those dark ages
of tears and despair.
There was nobody around
to take a picture.
Not enough light.

MY MOTHER

I don't see my mother
amongst the ancestors anymore.
She must be back on earth
as a little girl somewhere else.
Her new address must be there
in the akashic records,
but they don't allow me to see it.

It is now her life,
not mine or ours.

It is now my life,
not hers or ours.

LIFETIME

Time flew through my life
like a tornado.
Years swirled by
in the centrifuge of ages.

Now time is winding down.
Peace at last in this old ruin,
in this historic relic called the body

GOOD LUCK

M. was born with
a silver spoon in his mouth.
Sadly, over the years
the silver was tarnished
and the spoon bent beyond repair.

H. on the other hand was born
with a stainless steel spoon.
Now he is 80.
The spoon is still working
serving rich meals for others.

How would you define
what is good luck,
now or later?

LOST FUTURE

My aunt could foretell futures
from the coffee grounds at the bottom of a cup.
We children sat around her
believing that she was a wise one and a seer.

That future has come and gone.
It did not turn out as expected.
My aunt's new coffee maker
does not tell her anything.

I woke up.
I prefer this bleak morning,
breakfast in bed, instant coffee,
instant present.

LESSON

Time becomes a hard lesson.
How can I be so sure
that my life's cup is still half full?

Middle age was a promise
that there would be another age after.
Saturn tells me to stop and slow down.
Be frugal and don't waste!

If there is only a quarter of a cup left,
at least make it stronger!
Don't fool yourself and dilute it
with more water
to look fuller than it is.

In the end, an empty cup is no shame.

HOUSE OF BOOKS

Where is it written in my horoscope
that so many books
would come into my life
as friends and companions?

This amalgam called my soul is
many lifetimes old,
many nationalities old,
many religions old.
Who knows, but always books.

Don't take it literally!
The message is between the lines
or edited out
to be deciphered later.

THE GAME

The rules of the game have changed
but I am still playing.
If I dip my pen into coffee
the words may wake up.

A splash of ink on paper
can take many forms.
Imagination can take the form
of wisdom.

The mirror is the same as before,
but the cracks and wrinkles in the image
are recent.
I can't break the rules
of the end game.

THE JOURNEY

My birth certificate
was a one-way ticket
to an unknown destination.

Sometimes I took the wrong bus
or missed the train.
Hesitated at the crossroads
and was confused about the timetable.
Had recurring nightmares
about being lost.
My guardian angel had to work hard
to keep me on the right track.
Even so, I managed to travel
a long way.

One day the ticket will expire.
"Then", the astrologer predicted,
*"you will put your wings on
and take off to another plane."*

www.ingramcontent.com/pod-product-compliance
Lightning Source LLC
Chambersburg PA
CBHW071219070526
44584CB00019B/3072